Life
The Way It Was

Life
The Way It Was

Growing Up on a Clarendon Muckland Farm
in the 1940s and 1950s

Betty Sherwood Genter

Betty Sherwood Genter

VANTAGE Press

Cover design by Michael Fusco
Cover & interior illustrations by Betty Sherwood Genter
Interior design by Maria Fernandez, Neuwirth & Associates, Inc.
Vantage Press and the Vantage Press colophon
are registered trademarks of Vantage Press, Inc.

FIRST EDITION

Published by Vantage Press, Inc.

419 Park Ave. South, New York, NY 10016

Manufactured in the United States of America
ISBN: 978-0-533-16389-2
Library of Congress Catalog Card No: 2010908176
0 9 8 7 6 5 4 3 2 1

Foreword

GROWING UP ON A MUCKLAND FARM IN THE 1940S AND 1950s meant learning work and survival skills from parents. It meant learning what war was, and how it affected everyone's lives. Our small world became larger and the places we read about in school became places we might visit someday.

Hard work, common sense, energy and creativeness were needed in order to pay the bills and succeed. Everyone seemed to be strong, tough and extremely patriotic.

As you read the story of my experiences growing up, may they come alive in your mind, giving you a glimpse of what life was like then.

Acknowledgments

IN 2002, I WROTE THE ORIGINAL VERSION OF THIS WORK, *Growing up on a Clarendon Muckland Farm in the 1940s and 1950s*, for the Clarendon Historical Society. I was asked to do the project because I was still around and could remember what life was like then.

The muckland was slowly returning to its natural state of marshland, brush and woods. What was once a very productive area was becoming untillable and barren. The Historical Society had no history of this land in the township and wanted this gap in the town's history filled before it completely died away.

As I researched the material for the book, I found I was actually writing an autobiography of my early years of life. It would be difficult to separate the history from one's life at that time. As the work progressed, sub-themes emerged which were the signs of the times: hard work, values, and patriotism of the war years.

I now title this work, *Life: The Way It Was*.

Contents

Life
The Way It Was

Pearl Harbor

Sunday, December 7, 1941

I CAN REMEMBER THAT SUNDAY AFTERNOON, DECEMBER 7, 1941. We had recently moved into our home at 4578 Hindsburg Road in the town of Clarendon. I was in first grade in school. Most of the day was a typical Sunday. My father, brother, and I attended Mass at St. Mary's Church in Holley at 10:00 A.M. On the way home from church, we bought butter from the Smith's on Power Line Road. As children we liked it when it was time to buy butter because we had a chance to hear the Smith's brightly-colored parrot talk and whistle. When we arrived home, we ate Mom's chicken and biscuit dinner and played games on the living room floor all afternoon.

As evening approached, my father, Ray Sherwood, turned on the radio as usual for the evening news. President Roosevelt was speaking. He was announcing that the United States was at war. The Japanese had bombed Pearl Harbor. I couldn't comprehend what it all meant—only that it wasn't good. I remember my father and mother straining to hear all the details coming through the static and crackling, and the concerned looks on their faces. We three children knew enough to get very still and quiet so they could listen to the facts. There was also a discussion of whether or not my father would be drafted. The ending of that Sunday was not typical. A change in everyone's lives was about to happen.

Coping

LIKE MOST FARM FAMILIES WE DIDN'T HAVE MONEY FOR any extras, but we were pretty much self-sufficient. We raised pigs, chickens, ducks, turkeys and rabbits. My mother canned everything: meat, vegetables, and fruit. She baked most of her own bread. From our muckland farm we had plenty of potatoes, carrots, and onions and a big garden full of vegetables. Each winter we traded a pig for a quarter of beef. My father was a hunter so we often had wild game (rabbit, pheasant, and deer) to eat. He usually had two or three hunting dogs whom I befriended. I remember "Jack," "Blue," "Red," and "Smokey." I felt sorry for them tied out back to their individual houses with nothing to do. So I would feed and water them, talk with them and maybe crawl into their houses with them. That was before I knew anything about fleas and spiders.

Ray Sherwood was born on April 27, 1903 in Byron, New York to Harry and Anna Spahn Sherwood. While he was a young boy the family moved to Batavia, where he grew up at 211 Ross Street. As a young man he worked on the plumbing being installed in Attica prison when the prison was being built. He told my cousin, Lee Bowen, that his boss would show him and tell him what to do, then leave him alone to do it. When he returned and checked the work, if it wasn't done correctly, my father would have to tear it out and start all over. He said that is how he learned the plumbing trade. He paid attention and worked carefully so he didn't have to do any work over again.

My father worked for my grandparents and became a hunting partner with my uncle, Ray Bowen, and this is how he met my mother. He bought a chunk of woods in 1931 and started clearing it so he could raise crops. My mother was born June 19, 1905 to Fred and Grace Dolan Bowen on the Hulberton Road in Clarendon. They were married May 5, 1933 by the Rev. William Burckhardt in the rectory of St. Joseph's Church in Varysburg, New York.

Their firstborn was Gordon James, born April 22, 1934. He died of pneumonia three days before his first birthday, on April 19, 1935. Evarts & Salisbury funeral home in Holley prepared him for burial at a cost of $40.00. He was shown at my grandparent's home on Hulberton Road and buried on top of my grandfather's (Harry Sherwood's) grave in St. Joseph's Cemetery in Batavia. My grandfather had died shortly before and my parents didn't have the money for a separate grave. I can't begin to imagine the emotional impact this had on my mother who was pregnant with me. My parents had lost my mother's father, Fred Bowen, my father's father, Harry Sherwood, and their first born son, Gordon, within a year's time. I was born October 16, 1935. My brother, Carl, was born May 11, 1937, and my sister, Joyce, was born August 16, 1939.

Ray and Gladys Sherwood on their wedding day, 1933

Gladys and Ray Sherwood at their 25th wedding celebration, 1958

In 1939, my father came home with a 1937 red Chevy truck cab and frame. My mother and I watched out the window as he drove it up the driveway. He built the truck bed and racks and it became our only means of transportation for many years. After the war we purchased a 1938 Chevy sedan in which I learned how to drive. It became my car to drive to Brockport College from 1953 to 1956 and to work at Matthew's Ice Cream Dairy in Spencerport and Star Market in Brockport, where I was a cashier while attending college.

My father, Ray Sherwood, was known as a great hunter. He loved hunting raccoons. Bobby Brooks probably hunted with him more than anyone else. Bobby remembers when Ray first

TOP: August 1943—Betty, Carl, and Joyce Sherwood on the front porch with cats: Bobby and Fuzzie. BOTTOM: Easter 1946—Betty, Carl, and Joyce Sherwood with friends: Rabbit, Brownie the dog, Bobby the cat. Betty wearing new striped boys socks.

came to the Clarendon area with an old Dodge touring car from the 1920s. It had side curtains that had to be rolled up or down. When they went coon hunting the dogs sat in the back seat. If a deer was shot in season it was tied to the running board of the car. My only memory of that car was when it sat in our barn on the Hulberton Road, no longer drivable. I used to sit in it and pretend I was driving.

The Clarendon Grange Hall, formerly a hotel, had a pool table in one of the rooms. All the local men would hang out there in the evenings; especially in bad weather. Electricity in those days was a fleeting experience and service, as the slightest wind or storm would knock out the power. Whenever this happened, it didn't stop the pool players. They hung a lantern over the table and several along the sides of the room and the game continued. My father liked to play pool.

Bobby Brooks recalls a time when my father went to Pennsylvania with some friends. They lost their dogs and after looking extensively for them, had to come back to Clarendon without them. Two years later, my father received a post card saying someone in Pennsylvania had his dog. The dog tag gave the information on the owner. Ray was excited that this could be. After two years he was getting his lost dog back, but he was saddened when he got to Pennsylvania and heard that his friend's dog had been killed by a train. I have a post card my mother received from my father postmarked Williamsport, PA, October 24, 1934. It was written when he arrived the first time. It reads:

> Hello Gladys. I suppose you are wondering how we are. We arrived at 1:30 and hunted last nite but didn't hit a track & were in good country. George talked with 2 other hunters & they did not run any. Well here goes for tonight. The

> fellow where we are staying is quite a hunter—something like Uncle Bert as far as hunting is concerned. I suppose Gordon misses his daddy. So long.
>
> —Ray

My father was not one to show his emotions openly. We always thought of him as tough, strong, aloof, and independent. Finding this postcard gives us a closer, personal glimpse into the person we called, "Dad."

Ray belonged to the Black North Rod and Gun Club and the Batavia Sportsman's Club. My mother took the three of us to some of the field trials south of Batavia when we were older. In a field trial a bag of scent or an actual animal was put in a bag and dragged through the woods for a long distance, then secured high up in a tree. My father was usually the one who did the dragging and putting of the bag into the tree. All the hunters tried to have the best dog and this was a test. The hunters' dogs were let loose. The first dog to reach the tree and bark made his owner very proud and the winner.

Bobby Brooks recalls that raccoons sometimes got caught high up in the crotch of a tree when they were shot. Ray would put a chain around the tree and work himself up the tree to free the dead coon.

One night while coon hunting, my father tripped over a root, fell, and broke his hip. I remember him being in traction in his bed at home. When he was allowed to put some weight on it and walk with crutches, it was deer season. He was anxious to be outside and go hunting. Bob Harling went with him to Power Line Road and dropped him off by a long line of sugar maple trees, while he joined others to drive the woods.

As my father was leaning on his crutches with his back against the tree, he looked up and saw a huge buck coming toward him. With much difficulty he was able to lift and sight his gun and shoot the deer. This was probably one of the most often told hunting stories. His hunting buddies were at our house often, and we heard all the tales over and over. We could even finish some of them before the storyteller as we listened from the next room. Some of my father's hunting partners were: Claude Brooks, Bobby and Billy Brooks, Ray Bowen (my uncle), George Heisler, Bob Harling, Joe McFarland, Frank Thorpe, and Cleo Turner. Another friend, was Harold Morse, a huge, strong man from Batavia, who drove a gasoline truck out of Griegsville, New York.

My earliest memories come from the tenant house on Hulberton Road which my grandparents owned and where we lived for the first five years of my life. I remember my mother holding and rocking me many nights as I cried and cried. She would sit in a rocking chair, in the dark, as we had no electricity, and try to get me to go to sleep—often falling asleep herself. Now I know

Ray Sherwood with Dodge Touring Car from the '20s and deer hunting

TOP: Ray in 1939 with dog, Blue, and some racoon hides on side of tenant house on Hulberton Road. BOTTOM: Ray in 1950s with two hunting dogs behind house on Hindsburg Road.

I cried because of pain in my left hip. When I started to walk I would fall down a lot and cry, so I was taken to doctors in Rochester. X-rays showed that there was no ball and socket joint for my left hip; just rough bone moving against bone each time I moved my leg, causing pain. They called it a dislocated hip, put a cast on, and I had to stay in the hospital for at least two weeks. I can remember the iron hospital crib and my grandmother coming to visit me. She brought me a beautiful burgundy-colored cardigan sweater she had knitted. Both my grandmothers told my mother that I cried, and begged them to take me home to Mom, Dad, and Kitty, and that they couldn't stand to see me in there. After I was released from the hospital, I had to wear a heavy body cast on my left side to hold the hip in place, while tissue and muscle grew around it. The doctors told my parents I probably would not walk or go to school. If I did learn, I would have to be tutored at home. At clinics my parents were told I shouldn't walk, swim, or ride a bike. Now we know exercise is good. I continued to grow and started half-day kindergarten in the Stone School in Clarendon, which my mother had attended. Sometimes I had to walk the half mile from school to our home on the Hulberton Road when my father was working. I would be exhausted, but I did it. With a younger brother and sister I felt I had to be better, stronger, and faster than they were because I was the oldest.

My mother told me that the happiest years of her ninety-five years of life were when she and my father were first married and we three children were all under five years of age. This was when we lived in my grandparent's tenant house with no electricity and no inside plumbing. At this time my parents were clearing their muckland and raising a few acres of crops. My father did plumbing and worked for the town in winter. My mother always worked side by side with my father and we were there with them when we were little. My mother loved flowers and animals. We always had large flower beds around the house, chickens, and a cat, as well as my father's hunting dogs. Mother delighted in catching chipmunks, keeping them in cages as pets, and watching their antics. Once my brother climbed a tree in our woods and snatched a baby crow from its nest. My mother named it "Jennie" and fussed with it a lot. When we went to work on the muck, the crow followed us, swooping down and landing on our backs while we were crawling along, pulling weeds. We would put breadcrumbs in our pockets and the crow would peck at the pockets to get them. When work was finished the crow flew home and beat us there. One day the crow wasn't around. My mother called and called her. Then she heard a gunshot. She went into the woods and found two hunters who had shot "Jennie." They said they didn't know it was a pet, even though it was following them and was very friendly.

A highlight of the day for me, in good weather, when I was little, would be when my father would let me ride on his shoulders from the house to the well by the barn as he carried water to the house for cooking and washing clothes. My father was six-foot-two inches tall and I was sure I was able to see the whole world from his shoulders.

In our first home we lived in three rooms. The kitchen had a wood cook stove, a sink with a mirror over it where my father shaved with a straight razor and strop, a pantry, a table and chairs. A woodshed was off the back. We had to go through the woodshed to the outhouse in the backyard. My parents' bedroom held their bed, a dresser, and a baby crib for my sister. The main room (originally the dining room), held a pot-bellied stove, a dining room table, chairs, buffet, a crib for my brother, and a small day bed, which was used as a couch during the day and served as my bed at night. There was a front bedroom and living room, but they were only used in summer because there was no central heating. The upstairs had two tiny bedrooms, unused except for storage. Once, when Joyce was learning to walk, we were playing around the stove, weaving in and out among the wet clothes and chairs. She fell against the hot stove and severely burned her arm from wrist to elbow. I helped hold her while my mother changed the dressing twice a day and put ointment on it. It was a bad burn, but it healed completely and to this day there is no scar from it. Back then, people didn't have money to go to the doctor and instead became their own doctors.

My bed, or couch, was in front of a window, which looked out onto a side porch. One moonlit night, I was awakened by noises and turned over to look out the window. There on the porch were several of my grandparents' sheep, stomping around and bleating, making a huge racket with their feet on the wooden boards of the porch. One had his face up against the window glass and was looking back at me. I became terrified of sheep after this experience and it took many years for me to overcome my fear of all sheep.

With no telephone, my mother would sometimes write a note to her mother and send me as messenger, through the orchard between our house and grandma's. Sheep, cows, and a bull were pastured in the orchard. I was always told to stay behind trees and to look out for the bull. One day he chased me and I narrowly escaped through the fence, out of breath and scared. That day, grandma walked with me along the roadside when it was time to go back home.

Records in the Town Clerk's office in Clarendon show that in 1910 the far eastern muckland (then swampland) was purchased by Clark D. Webster, Milford Salisbury, and Frank Potter. This area, between South Manning Road east to Upper Holley Road, was mostly owned by the Webster and Robinson families from the 1940s through the 1990s. The Manning muck on the south end of Hindsburg Road in the 1930s through the 1950s had been parceled into smaller units of acreage.

Family records show that on October 3, 1931, twenty-seven acres of uncleared swampland was bought by Raymond Sherwood. He had a $1000 mortgage from FDIC (Federal Deposit Insurance Corporation). The twenty-seven acres were part of Lot #228, Township 3 and part of the larger 100,000 acre tract, or Connecticut Tract. These twenty-seven acres are located on the north eastern edge of the Alabama Swamp on Hindsburg Road in the Town of Clarendon. It was also known as the "Manning Muck." The parcels to the east of South Manning Road were known as the "Clarendon Muck." In 1879, Lot #228 was owned by Benjamin Pettingill; in 1891 by Orville P. Turner; in 1927 by Mary Salisbury; and in 1931 by John Langham (who sold it to Ray Sherwood).

The owners of parcels in the Manning Muck in the forties and fifties were, starting at the north end of the west side of Hindsburg Road, Henry Stymus, James & William Gaylord, Rudy & Fritz Brant, Pete Bowen, Irving Kennedy, Al Pilato, Fred & Ray Bowen, and John Mansfield.

Starting at the north end of the east side of Hindsburg Road, land was owned by Ray Sherwood, John & Ed Murphy, David Bridgeman, and William Copeland. Through the years Pelligrino Brothers and Tony DelPlato bought out most of the smaller owners.

As the trees and stumps were removed, crops of lettuce, onions, carrots, potatoes, and cabbage were planted in the rich black soil. My mother and father cleared most of our fifteen to twenty acres of tillable land by hand when they were first married and when we were babies. At times the stumps were blasted out with dynamite.

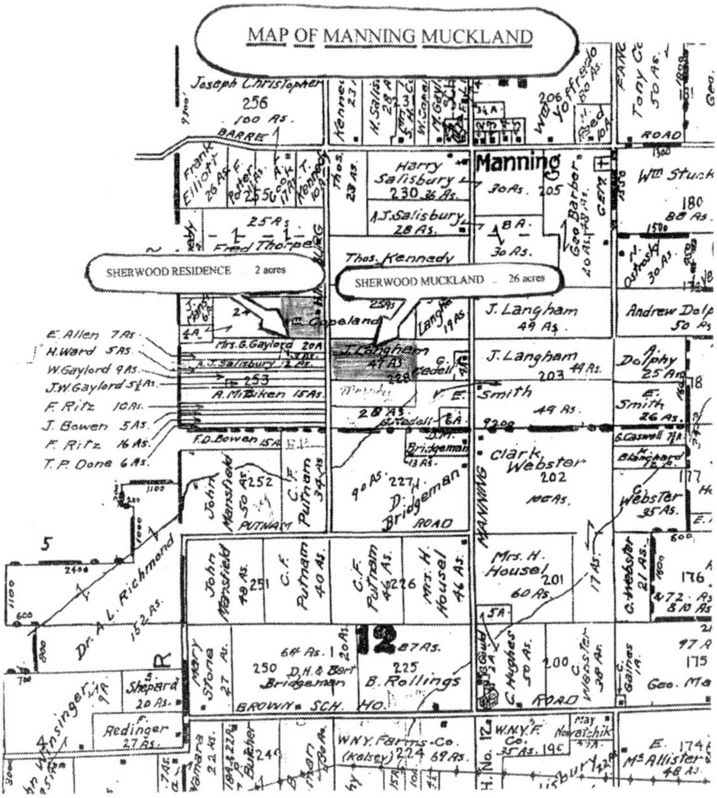

An article written by Henry Greffrath in *The Standard Cyclopedia of Horticulture*, copyright 1900, reprinted 1937, p. 2074, gives a description on the tilling and handling of muckland:

> There are many different opinions as to how muck should be tilled. Some growers believe in deep plowing so as to get the best of conditions possible for a good root-growth. However, deep plowing should never be practiced in the spring. If virgin muck soil is brought to the surface in spring

> or summer, it will bake and form lumps much like soft coal, and will not do well. The deep plowing should be done in the fall after the frost has worked on the virgin subsoil which when brought to the top becomes pulverized and will be in fine condition for dropping the next spring. When the frost is out of the ground in the spring, break up the soil thoroughly with a cultivator to a depth of six inches, and put on the first application of fertilizer. Work this well into the soil by dragging it three or four times and then go over the land with a leveler after which the seed is sown.
>
> Deep cultivation in early spring helps to dry out the soil and warms it up, and causes the roots of the crop to work deeply into the ground. As the crops grow and the weather and soil warm up, cultivation must be continued, but of less depth so that roots are not cut off. If shallow cultivation is practiced at first, the root-growth will all be near the surface and when dry weather sets in, roots will have no moisture and the plants stop growing until they can send roots down into moist soil. A mulch of dry muck for a depth of one or 2 inches will carry the crop through a dry spell in good condition. In wet weather the land should be left in ridges after cultivating, as this helps to dry it. In dry weather, however, it should be left as level as possible in order to hold the moisture.

The weather reports on radio and the predicting of weather conditions became very important to those who worked muckland.

Muckland farmers were often forced to borrow money from low interest loan companies, such as Production Credit, after a year or two of losing their crops to wind, flooding, drought, or insects. The loans enabled them to purchase seed, fertilizer, and equipment to start all over again. We bought seeds from Vick's and Harris Seed Company; seed potatoes from C. Webster, Frank Yaskulski, and Marky Brothers in Elba.

As children of muck farmers we learned at an early age how to drive a tractor and truck, how to fill the baskets or crates on a potato or onion picker, how to stack three crates together, how to weed three or five rows of plants at a time, and how to mix chemicals with water for spraying the crops. We also knew the names of the different varieties of potatoes, carrots, and onions. I remember my father liked to raise Essex and Katahdin potatoes, Chatenay Coreless carrots, and Yellow Globe onions.

Once the crops came up they had to be sprayed and weeds pulled several times during the summer. It was a never-ending job. Harvesting of onions was at the end of August and the first part of September. Potatoes and carrots followed in October and November. I recall one November, before Thanksgiving, when we were harvesting carrots. I must have been eight years old. It was snowing, blizzard-like, as I helped put covers on baskets of carrots and then covered them with the discarded carrot tops

ABOVE: Carl, Joyce and Brownie in our potato field in August.
ALL OPPOSITE: Joyce, Carl, and Myrtie Pratt in our onion field in August.

to keep them from freezing. I was so very cold and wet; so was everyone else . . . we had to save the crop.

Children of muck farmers knew their value as free labor for working and harvesting the crop with their parents. In the summer, after all of our parent's crops were weed-free, we could work for a neighbor and get paid. This lasted from one to two weeks, until we were needed back on the home plot, to crawl or walk over every foot of land and pull all the weeds again. This was usually done three or four times throughout the summer. My father would hire any neighborhood teen who was available to work. This was a fun time for me. To have someone to laugh and talk with made the tedious job of weeding go by faster. I especially liked having Clayton and Roy Bubb as work buddies.

We discussed how we would end our favorite comic strips (*Blondie, Lil' Abner, Dick Tracy*), types of vacation homes we would like to own, our future hopes and dreams, and laughed a lot. We even shot a few onions at each other and with a little encouragement from others, I would cavort around with two big onions in the front of my work shirt. At twelve years old this was hilariously entertaining and for a few years I, as a skinny, flat-chested teen, was known as "Betty Boobs" . . . even more ridiculous, but funny.

My mother, Gladys Sherwood, kept a ledger for each year. She wrote down what was spent for every item bought and for every expense encountered. Under the heading of "Labor " for 1951, a section on page 32 shows that various people worked on days when they could and that they were paid by the day or week. The ones who worked by the day were teenagers. Charlie Heller was a pretty steady employee who worked by the week. It reads:

June	2	Earl Norton	$6.30
	5	Charles Heller	41.88
	8	Lois Bubb	12.00
	9	Staryl Bridgeman	18.00

9	Clayton Bubb	15.00
9	Cecil Moore	12.00
9	June Campbell	6.00
9	Richard Belair	6.00
16	Charlie Heller	35.65
23	Charlie Heller	29.62
26	June Campbell	12.00
27	Staryl Bridgeman	10.50
27	Woodrow Baker	23.26
30	Charles Heller	24.80

Making a decent living was difficult on a muck farm. For every good year of produce and income, chances are you would have two or three bad ones. In 1950 they didn't even break even. My mother's ledger shows the following on pages 24 and 25:

Expenses 1950		**Cash Receipts 1950**	
Labor hired	$350.76	10710# Carrots	
Gasoline, oil, fuel	304.99	@ 23.00 T.	$128.52
Supplies	82.88	7 ducks	6.54
Repairs & Mainten.	190.02	Compensation	64.00
Truck & Auto	187.14	6 Geese	19.76
Interest on mortgage	104.00	Plumbing	42.00
Seeds	97.73	Refunds	40.48
Fertilizer	367.75	Potatoes (270)	308.05
Dust & spray	125.90	Labor—Jobs	530.49
Storage	300.00	Truck work, potato	
Snow fence posts	22.00	digging	82.00
Taxes	74.53	Carrots—56 T.	798.29
Poultry feed	409.65	Chickens—33	51.23
Sawing crate slats	32.40	Ducks—37	45.63
Harvesting onions	83.00	Geese—11	40.76
Turkeys—3	4.50	Eggs—1011 Doz.	414.29
Doctor bills	6.00		
Charity	23.00	Cash	$ 2406.02
Expenses	$2766.25		

Summers were unbearable to me. Most muck farms had hedgerows of willows separating different sections. They were planted as windbreaks to protect the seed, fertilizer and small plants from being blown away by the wind. In summer, the black soil collected and held the heat and the willows prevented any movement of air. The hot, humid air made it difficult to breathe as you crawled on your hands and knees up and down the rows, pulling weeds.

Muckland has different characteristics than loam farmland. Because it consists of decayed plant material it is very fertile for growing vegetables. However, once it gets saturated with rain it becomes soup. I recall one October when I was in college, wanting to spend a weekend at the college camp in the Adirondack Mountains, but there was no money. I had to earn the twenty dollars somehow, I would rush home from classes in the afternoon, change my clothes, and run to Bill Gaylord's muck and work as fast as I could filling crates with potatoes for ten cents a crate. One day it began raining hard and I kept on working; throwing potatoes into the crates. Within a short time, I was crawling and wading in black soup up to my knees. The suction was so great I had a difficult time pulling up one foot at a time to exit the potato field to harder, dryer land. By the way, I did earn the money and had a great weekend at camp.

I once lost my boots in a bog hole on our land. It was spring and warm and I was roaming the woods next to the cleared muckland. I often hiked the woods and fields and this particular day I was picking flowers and looking for pussy willows. I left the woods, crossed a brushy area and started across an area of muck to get to the wooded area on the other side. About halfway across the black muck, I began to sink in with each step. I tried to go back, but couldn't. I was stuck.

I couldn't move. The more I tried, the more I sank further into the hole. I wondered if this was the same as quicksand. Finally, I pulled my feet from my boots and managed to walk the half-mile home barefooted. I remember collapsing on the couch and sleeping for a long time. The area where I lost my boots dried out. Summer came and went. We often looked for my boots. They were never found, even after plowing the land the next year.

Fighting the Bugs

IN ORDER TO RAISE A GOOD CROP, MOST FARMERS HAD TO dust or spray the seedlings several times as they grew. Before 1950 this was a big operation by hand. In the '50s airplanes took over for the large farmers. The double-winged crop dusters could fly in and out of the hedgerows, just missing the trees and electric wires. Such skill! Watching a pilot maneuver his plane to a few feet above the ground, let out a cloud of dust or spray, then shoot almost straight up over the treetops, became a favorite summer pastime for us. A local pilot, Chuck Mansfield, lived to the south of us at the end of Hindsburg Road and around the corner. He flew in World War II. After the war he died when his plane crashed in a southern state.

Prior to the airplane (crop duster), we had to mix liquid or powdered poisons into barrels of water which had been pumped from the ditches. Names such as: Blue Vitro, formaldehyde, and Arsenic come to mind. I used to help my father mix the chemicals into the water in the drums. Then I would have to stir each drum with a long wooden stick. I often wonder if my sensitivity to chemicals started back then. One day, in a nearby shed where we stored supplies and equipment, I saw a dead bird on the ground. My father said it must have eaten some of the Blue Vitro sitting on the rafters. He warned us never to get any of it on our hands or face. At that instant I realized how toxic and deadly

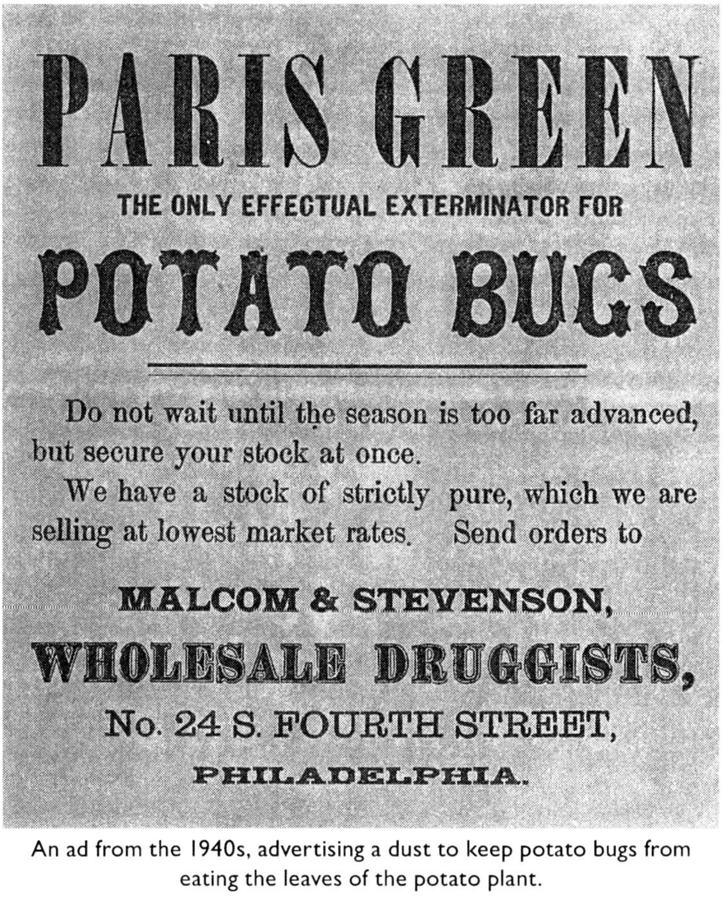

An ad from the 1940s, advertising a dust to keep potato bugs from eating the leaves of the potato plant.

TOP: Mixing chemicals for spraying the crops.
BOTTOM: Potato harvesting equipment: Cletrac tractor, pulling digger, pulling picker with crates to be filled with potatoes.

these chemicals were. Of course, without them, there would be no harvest.

Successful Farming, copyright 1944, vol. 1, No. 4, p. 40–41, provides an Insect Control Chart. You can look up the crop, then the insect, then a formula is listed to eliminate the pest. In another section the contents of the formulas and how to mix them are given. In another place are disinfectants and formulas for animal problems such as "Dips for Cattle and Sheep, Scab and Mange and Lice on Hogs." My mother had a notebook with many of these formulas she used, written out with notes on the best way to apply. There were also medicine recipes from my grandmother. One was a black salve that would heal just about anything, especially deep cuts.

Harvesting

USUALLY THE FIRST AND SECOND WEEKS IN SEPTEMBER were prime harvest time for onions. Since this was also the beginning of school, parents often kept their children home to help with the harvest. My brother, Carl, had to do this for a few days when he was a teen. More often than not, we went to school during the day, then started working on the onion picker in the afternoon and through the evening until midnight or after. The tops of the onions cut better at night. Most farmers topped onions by hand with sheep shears into the 1950s, but one by one, bigger farmers bought harvesting machines to shorten harvest time. Smaller farmers would hire a farmer with a machine to do their harvesting also. When I was twelve years old and my brother, Carl, was ten, we worked together as a team, topping onions with sheep shears for a neighbor at ten cents a bushel. We started at 7:00 A.M. and finished at 6:00 P.M. By the end of the day we had topped 110 bushels of onions and had made $5.50 each. We thought we were rich. We were told that we had topped more than any of the other adults who were working that day—we had set a record.

An empty crate would be pulled between us as we scooped up a bunch of onions with our left hands. Holding the bunch over the crate, we would quickly snip off the tops of the onions and they would fall into the crate. The sheep shears were always kept razor-sharp. One day as I was working I noticed blood running down my left hand and arm. Upon examination, I found that I had snipped off the knuckle on my left thumb. I had not felt any stinging or pain. When I went home, I washed it and my mother bandaged it up and I went back to work.

Weather determined the hours and days of harvest. Rain meant hundreds or thousands of bushels of onions sitting in the wet soup. The goal was a get the onion crates stacked, then picked up, and finally stored in a dry place. If harvested on rainy days the crates of onions would have to dry out before hauling them to storage. A few muck farmers sold some of their crop from the field, but most, including my parents, stored the produce in storage buildings with fans until the market price in winter was a lot higher than it was in the fall. Page 63 of my mother's ledger, under "Cash Receipts 1952," lists the amount of produce sold and the amount of money received:

Onions (3600 bu.)	$7,490.60
Potatoes (2008 crates)	3,934.75
Carrots (65 ton)	666.96

We stored our onions and potatoes in a storage building on my grandparent's farm on the Hulberton Road. Sometimes two or three farmers got together and helped each other harvest, especially if the weather had been bad. I remember hauling truckloads of onions and potatoes to the storage, three miles away in Clarendon. Sometimes, the kids rode way up on top of the load. This was fun. Once when I was fourteen or fifteen (still without a driving license, but having driven the truck and tractor all over our land) I was told I had to drive a truck, loaded with onions, to the storage three miles away—the weather looked bad. There was no traffic on the roads. Oh, how carefully I drove and when I successfully delivered the load, I remember the feeling of being trusted with responsibility, doing adult's work, and contributing to the finances of the family. It was just expected of us. I knew I was growing up.

Most farmers repaired their own equipment and helped their neighbors with repairs. Through all my growing up years, we had the trusty 1937 Chevy truck. If it needed fixing, Bud Callard in Clarendon did the work. If we needed a part to be welded, Otis Bartlett in Manning did it. Those who had harvest machines often shared with those who didn't. My father bought the parts for his potato picker from a catalog and assembled it himself, with the help of my brother, Carl. It was usually my brother and me who stood on the narrow platforms (one on each side) of the picker and picked off the bunches of potato vines as they came up the conveyor belt with the potatoes. It was quite an operation to watch potato harvesting with this new invention. No more crawling on hands and knees to pick up potatoes by hand.

First in line was the tractor, followed by the digger. Hooked to the digger was the picker. As the potatoes were dug, they were carried by a conveyor belt of metal links and fell onto the picker—vines and all. The people standing on the side platforms would throw off any rotten potatoes, sticks, stones, and vines; on the back of the picker was a platform which held another person and bunches of stacked, empty crates. The person standing on the platform at the rear had the most important job. Two crates were sitting side by side under the conveyor belt. There was a board which could be flipped as a gate so only one crate would receive potatoes. When one crate was filled, the board was flipped to the other side, the full crate was set on the ground, and a new empty crate was placed under the belt. All this while the tractor slowly pulled the digger and the picker along the hilled rows of potatoes.

I looked forward to the time when I would be strong enough to lift a crate of potatoes to the ground and get back on the platform while this "train" of equipment moved like a snail down one row after another. I don't remember being able to do it. It took muscles and I was a skinny kid. Strong, but not that strong.

Life Then

MOST MUCK FARMERS HAD OTHER JOBS TO SUPPORT THEIR families and pay the bills. My father was a plumber. Many area farmers, both dairy and muck farmers, sought him out to install or repair pumps. Gordis's Hardware in Holley was where he bought most of his plumbing supplies and where he was often given names by Earl Gordis and Oren VanOrden of farmers who needed work done. People were beginning to want indoor bathrooms and water piped to their kitchens. When I was fourteen, my father gave us the luxury of inside plumbing—a bathroom and water to the kitchen sink. No more cold trips to the outhouse. Prior to this we carried drinking and cooking water from a well off our property, which was at least two hundred feet from our house. A pump, in the kitchen near the sink, provided cistern water for bathing and washing clothes and dishes.

From a ledger my mother kept, the best year of all was 1953—the year I graduated from high school and started college. We rented extra muckland, the weather cooperated, we had a wonderful harvest, and the prices were good. The total amount of money taken in from the sale of crops, eggs, and plumbing was $14,792.27. The total expenses and bills came to $7456.58. They were finally getting up in the world. They bought the only new car we ever had: a 1953 Chevrolet sedan, for $2129.25. Also, a freezer for $340.00, and a safe for $62.00. Probably they put their extra money in the safe; at least part of it. My father would keep the old 1938 Chevy running for three more years so I could drive it to Brockport

SPECIAL DEFENSE MESSAGE

to American Farmers

From

Donald Danforth, President, PURINA MILLS

As this issue of Better Farms Magazine goes to press, Lend Lease purchases of food for Britain will be running over $2,000,000 a day. The government's 1942 farm program designed to provide the largest supply of food ever produced in this country in a single year will be well under way. Yes, America is today not only the arsenal of Democracy, but also the bread-basket. »»«« Meat, Milk, and Eggs are as necessary to win this war as guns, ships, and planes. Never before has the American Farmer had a greater responsibility or a greater opportunity to defend his country and aid mankind. »»«« It is not my purpose to urge you to increase the size of your herds or flocks, though if that is possible by all means do so. But I do want to say that if you ever did a good job of turning pullets into layers — do it now. If you ever raised big hogs quickly — do it now. If you ever fed dry cows and milk cows for long life and heavy production — do it now. »»«« The feeding and management programs recommended by Purina Mills are, as thousands of farmers can testify, most effective. As a livestock or poultry feeder, you are entitled to the expert feeding advice the trained Purina personnel can give you. No matter what your feeding problems may be, go to see your local Purina dealer, or write to Purina Mills, Buffalo, N. Y. »»«« This year runts, non-layers, and low producers are unpatriotic as well as unprofitable. Let's keep America's bread-basket full. Let's Fight by Producing.

Donald Danforth

PURINA MILLS

BUFFALO, N. Y.

An example of a patriotic ad from a flour mill in Buffalo in 1942, urging farmers to produce for the war effort.

College. In 1954 we got a black and white TV (color wasn't around yet). In 1956 we had a telephone installed. Sometime between 1954 and 1956, my father put baseboard heat in our house. No more loading the wood and coal stoves, carrying wood and coal from the basement, or taking out the ashes.

The first few years of the 1940s (the war years) were difficult for most families. This was true in things other than food and feeding the family. There was rationing of sugar and gasoline. If you were a farmer you were allowed extra gasoline stamps. You also got a refund at the end of the year for the gasoline tax you had paid during the year if you were a farmer.

Businesses and factories put out literature and ads supporting the war effort. One such company was The Spool Cotton Company. It published a booklet entitled, *Make and Mend for Victory*, copyright 1942. It was a guide to alterations, make-overs, mending and darning, with diagrams and pictures to help women make use of all their family's existing clothing. On the first page is a pledge, which reads:

CONSUMER'S VICTORY PLEDGE:

"As a consumer, in the total defense of democracy, I will do my part to make my home, my community, my country ready, efficient, strong.

I will buy carefully—and I will not buy anything above the ceiling price, no matter how much I may want it.

I will take good care of the things I have—and I will not buy anything made from vital war materials which I can get along without.

> **I will waste nothing**—and I will take care to salvage everything needed to win the war."

A little further along it states:

> It's up to you to keep the home fires burning, to see that you and your family stay easy-on-the-eyes. Fortunately, you can be patriotic and pretty both. It's easy to teach an old wardrobe new tricks, to resurrect the skeletons in your closet and bring them up to date. Come on, take those old knockabouts and turn them into knockouts, keep that glint in Uncle Sam's eye and still do your stint towards Victory!

Niagara-Hudson Power Company produced a booklet, *Healthy Americans*, by Margaret E. Bicknell, copyright 1942, giving suggestions on how to plan meals wisely, how to purchase foods wisely, how to preserve and store foods, and how to feed the family. Again, patriotism is part of the message on page 3:

> You are pretty proud of America and Americans, aren't you? Of course you are and so am I, but I'll admit I was appalled and a bit ashamed when I read that about one-third of the young men called up for military service were rejected for physical defects due either directly or indirectly to nutritional deficiencies. Isn't that amazing, in a country such as ours with all the vast kinds and quantities of foods available to fit any income, and surplus food and food stamps for those without any income. Let us see if we can't change that figure.

My mother helped get extra money by raising chickens and rabbits. I helped her load the trunk and back seat of the 1938 Chevy after supper on Friday and Saturday nights in the summer. We would drive to Hulberton and slowly drive along the main road and stop in front of the houses. The Italian men and women would come running out to see what we had. We always sold everything. They liked fresh meat they could dress themselves. I didn't like to let go of my rabbits—my pets—but I knew we had too many to feed and we needed the money.

Because I had worn a heavy body and leg cast at one-and-a-half years old, my vertebrae were all pulled out of their normal place by the weight of the one-sided cast when I was growing fast. The curvature of my spine was discovered when a doctor visited the school and checked everyone. A letter was given to me to give to my parents. My parents had to decide what, if anything, they would do. I ended up going to Joseph Fiorito, a chiropractor, in Fancher, two times a week for six years. He put all the vertebrae back in place and helped me to grow up tall and straight. Each visit cost my parents $2.00. Four extra dollars a week was a lot of money to spend on one kid. Some how they managed. In my growing years I always had pain, but lived with it and was able to do just about anything I wanted to. And, school became my whole life. I guess I proved all the doctors wrong.

To our north lived our nearest neighbors, Fred and Maude Thorpe. They were elderly when we were young. They always had sheep, one or two cows, a horse, and chickens. Maude was a tiny, energetic, creative woman. She made her own hats and even won a prize at the county fair for one of her designs. Fred was older and chewed tobacco. As children we liked to watch him spit tobacco juice at the spittoon near his chair. When he missed, Maude would clean it up.

Fred used to come down to the ditches of the Manning Muck to fill his spray rig. Ethelyn Clark recalls one time when she was helping her brother, Irving, and father, Lawrence Kennedy, on the muck when Fred was filling his rig with water. He had hired Alf Gaylord just to hang on to the horses while he was pumping the water. The horses got scared and started to run away. Irving and Lawrence ran after them and finally caught them. Fred was all upset as he told Irving and Lawrence, "Don't you fellows ever tell Maude about them running away; especially after I hired Alf to hang on to them."

The Thorpes had a huge cream separator in their kitchen, which Maude used to make butter, cream, and buttermilk. Sometimes I was allowed to turn the crank handle. Each spring, Fred would hire Bill Gaylord or anyone else with a truck, to take his lambs to the train station in Holley. Here, the sheep and lambs were loaded on the train and shipped to Buffalo for slaughter. The Thorpe's sold their farm to Sherwood and Ethelyn Clark and moved into Bill Copeland's house on 31A. A few years later they moved to Upper Holley Road where Fred died. Maude spent her remaining years in a retirement home in Rochester.

Brothers David and Dudley Mathes bought a 118-acre farm for $3500 on East Lee Road (31A). David and Helen Mathes were married in 1943 and lived on the farm the first years of their marriage. Dudley was drafted and joined the Navy. The shortage of labor was a real challenge at this time as all the young farm boys were being drafted. Helen Mathes recalls:

> The first winter we were still using horses. We started out with eight Shorthorns and sold milk to Keople's cheese factory in Clarendon. We shared farming with David's

parents who lived near by. The summer of 1944 we acquired a baler and our first tractor, an Allis-Chalmers C. We also had a chicken house out back. I raised some broilers and had good luck selling them. We decided an indoor bathroom was one of our priorities. David dug a hole for a septic tank. I remember carrying water by the pailful across the road from a well by the barn to make the cement. A neighbor (Ray Sherwood) was able to get the tub and fixtures for us and do the piping. Soon after we had finished it we had a Grange Card Party. One hundred people came. David had to prop up the floor. I think they came to see the bathroom as they were still a novelty in the country.

Our horses were named Trixie and Dick. The winter of 1944, I would ride Trixie up the Road (31A) to the west and deliver all the mail to the neighbors. Clarendon was able to plow their roads, but the town of Barre was snowed in for six weeks. Barre couldn't get parts to fix their plows due to World War II. The next summer, David's father bought a Ford Tractor and plow for $985. It was soon decided we didn't need the horses anymore, so they were sold and I was very unhappy. We started separating our milk and selling the cream to Farmount Creamery in New York City. About this time we were able to buy our first refrigerator at the Firestone Store in Albion. On the farm we grew mostly hay and wheat and a few acres of beans. The next summer, 1945, we raised chickens to sell eggs. We would sell eggs by the case (30 doz.) to Kirby Motel on Ridge Road near Rochester for $15.24 a case. One year we sold hatching eggs to Newhouser Hatchery on West Avenue in Batavia.

> We did not have much leisure time. The Grange played a big part in our lives at that time. We were members of the Barre Center Grange, but Clarendon and Gaines had active organizations also. All three Granges held square dances on different Saturday nights. I remember listening to President Roosevelt's fireside chats. Our families were mostly Republican so they did not think much of Roosevelt. I saw him once before he was President in Rochester when our father took us to the fair. He came in and rode around in the back of a car. Dad said: "Take a good look at him because he will be the next President." On June 6, 1945 we went on the boat trip from Rochester to Colburg, Canada with friends, Clyde and Avis Downey. When we returned to Rochester, everyone was celebrating that the war was over.

David and Helen Mathes moved to the family farm on the Mathes Road and Dudley and Margaret took over the farm on 31A.

In late fall or winter several neighbors would plan a butchering day at one of the farms. Large kettles of water with hot wood fires underneath them were heated to boiling. Large hooks were attached above the barn doors and to trees to hang up the slaughtered animals. The animals were usually pigs, but once in awhile a calf or sheep would be included. On butchering day, I would walk from school to the Bubb farm where my father was helping. There were probably four other farmers there butchering their animals. Each helped the others. The first time I was allowed to walk there I was in a hurry. I couldn't wait to see this procedure. It was the only time I was curious.

As I approached the scene, the screams of the animals filled the air and my curiosity turned to disgust and sorrow for the animals. Instead of watching, I avoided the whole scene and headed for the house to play with my friends. The whole process of sticking, blood letting, scalding, scraping and cutting up the meat seemed to me a gory mess. Even though I knew this was our meat (pork) for the whole next year, the sight of all the blood and the screams of the animals lingered in my mind; even to this day. Even the entrails were cleaned by the women to be used as casings for sausage. Some neighbors made blood sausage; some made head cheese, but we didn't because we didn't like these products.

My mother always cooked the slabs of fat from the pig in the oven of the cook stove. The grease was poured into tin cans and put where it was cool in our pantry and basement. This gave Mom her cooking lard for pie crusts and frying. I can still smell the scent of grease that hung in the air of our house and on our clothes. I didn't like it.

The day after butchering, some of the boys would bring a part of the pig to school to taunt the girls. It might be the bladder, the tail, an eye, or a foot. They were successful at their taunting when we screamed and ran away.

We had a smokehouse out back of our house. It was made of stone and had a wooden roof and door. There were beams running across the middle and top with large hooks to hold the hams and slabs of bacon. A corncob fire was used to smoke them. After quite a few days of hanging in the smoke, we moved the meat to the upstairs back room of our house. If our job had been to keep the corncob fire going, our clothes reeked of smoke. No one at school seemed to notice or care because everyone smelled this way at least once a year. Pickled meat sat in crocks in the basement with the elderberry and grape wine, the rows of canned fruit and vegetables, the crates of potatoes, onions, and carrots. My mother used a recipe from my grandmother Sherwood for Elder Wine:

> 1 qt. of hulled elderberries
> 1 qt. of water. Boil until shriveled.
> When cool, add slice of fresh toast with 1 yeast cake on it.
> Let stand in warm place until through working.
> Bottle and store.

Survival in winter depended on keeping warm with the coal-burning potbellied stove in the living room and the wood-burning cook stove in the kitchen. We would undress around the living room stove, then run quickly upstairs and jump under the covers because there was no heat upstairs. On Saturday night, each took his/her turn in the kitchen to take a bath. Our house wasn't insulated when we were growing up and snow often blew in around the window edges. As children we had the never-ending task of keeping the coalscuttle and the wood box filled. The cook stove also had a water reservoir on the left side, which had to be filled with water. It provided us with warm to hot water for washing ourselves, and our dishes.

Once my parents told my brother to fill the reservoir and give water to the dogs as they left to work on our muck. Off the side porch was a well with a pump that we used for these two jobs. My brother was angry that he had to do these jobs—again. He lifted up the pump handle as far as he could and then slammed it down hard. The handle rebounded before he could move out of the way and it hit square between his eyes. He fell backward, landed on the porch floor, and blacked out for a few seconds. I found him and helped him to the couch.

I placed cool cloths on the huge "goose egg" that sprouted out between his eyes. We didn't have a refrigerator with ice. His whole face and both eyes became black and blue for at least two weeks.

My paternal grandmother was an excellent seamstress and often made clothes for me. She also collected clothes from people she worked for doing housework. In those days everyone wore hand-me-downs and didn't think about colors matching or how something fit. My grandmother would take an adult's wool coat apart and fashion a long winter coat and maybe a pair of leggings out of it. Actually, I never had a store-bought coat until I was a senior in high school. After saving money from my noon hour waitress job at Furman's Diner in Holley, two friends and I took the Greyhound bus from Holley to Rochester to go on a shopping spree. Both riding on a Greyhound bus and shopping in Rochester were first-time experiences for me as a school senior.

We were always needed. Some winters we had extra wood so the wood would have to be cut, split, and stacked. For several years we had a buzz saw with a gasoline engine sitting in our yard, which had become a wood lot. My father was able to sell the wood we didn't need for extra money to pay the bills. We used to play hide-and-seek among and around the stacked rows of wood.

Traveling for a vacation was unknown in the 1940s. Any travel consisted mostly of going to Floyd Gillis's Grocery Store for groceries or to the GLF for chicken feed, seeds, a shovel handle, or a small tool in Clarendon three miles away. Once a week, on Saturday night, we would drive the five miles to Holley to buy anything else we couldn't get in Clarendon. There we might be treated to a bottle of pop or an ice cream soda. If it was time to buy a pair of shoes or a special piece of clothing, we went to Albion, which was ten miles away. In the summers in the 1950s, we often piled into the 1938 Chevy after church on Sunday and headed for the hills of southern New York. We got to know the Finger Lake region well as we ate our picnic lunch in different locations along the way. I remember memorizing the routes we took and reading the map for my father. In the 1950s, I remember going to two Bowen family reunions at Hamlin Beach State Park. My parents went to Ohio and Michigan once and to New England once, in the late 1950s. These were the only trips taken while my father was alive. He died on October 4, 1962. When I started teaching in 1956, I had not been further west than Buffalo. Evenings were spent at home. I liked to listen to certain programs on the radio: *The Green Hornet*, *The Lone Ranger*, and *Inner Sanctum*.

I always wanted a bicycle, even though my parents were told by doctors when I was only a year old that I should not swim or ride a bike. Thank God my parents didn't have time to over-protect me from normal activities. When other neighbor children worked for my father on the muckland, they had bikes and taught me how to ride. We would practice in the road at lunchtime. When I was in sixth grade and my brother was in fourth grade, our father said if we kept track of the hours we worked during the summer and had earned enough (at $.60 per hour), he would buy us bicycles in the fall. The end of summer came and so did a beautiful blue Sterling bicycle. My brother had a shiny red one. I still have my blue Sterling.

We thought we were the luckiest, richest kids in the world. In the evenings we would race like the wind, around the country block—about 3 miles. On the route we were sure we were noticed by everyone. Sometimes we would stop and play ball or visit. The next few years saw these bikes taking us to new territories, new jobs, and new adventures. Greatest of these was heading for the Bubb's cow pasture to play baseball as soon as spring had really settled in for good. We knew there would always be others over there to play with. Another place we went was to the Gaylord's on Friday night to watch boxing and wrestling; riding the mile home, late at night, with just the tiny headlight on our bike to light the way. You see, the Gaylord's were the first to get a TV. That fall their home became a gathering place for the local teenagers. They didn't seem to mind having the house filled with teen bodies wall to wall. Our bicycles also took us cherry-picking for a few days in July when we weren't needed at home to work. The money earned bought school supplies and clothes and gave us spending money for the county fair.

Once when I was thirteen, I told my mother I wanted to take a day's journey by myself on my bicycle. She didn't have any objections so I packed my lunch and started off. I found out that twenty miles on a bike was a hard journey. I made it to Albion and back, but from then on, I was content with shorter treks nearer to home. During my growing-up years the fields and woods were my playground. Once we had bicycles, my brother and I fashioned paths and trails through these fields and woods and would ride over them at high speed. Once I didn't duck for a low-hanging branch soon enough. The branch hit me in the nose and I fell backward off my bike. After that I went a little slower and watched out for obstacles in my path. To this day I have a slight bump on the ridge of my nose as a reminder.

In winter we often were snowed in for one or two weeks. There would be no way to get to school and I hated it. I always wanted to be in school. Only the main roads were opened at first after a storm and the plows then were not built to buck a

The cover of a 1935 Burpee's seed catalog. Gladys Sherwood ordered flower and garden seeds by mail.

solid drift many feet high. Eventually, a crew of volunteer men would come with the snowplow and clean out the snow by hand with shovels, leaving a one-lane track through the drifts. At times my father helped clear the roads after a storm had passed. I don't know if he volunteered or was paid. One time we were running out of supplies so my father took a burlap bag, dressed warmly, and walked across fields to the main road, where he hitch-hiked to Holley. He probably had cabin fever and had to get out.

Actually, we were an outdoor family. No matter what the weather was we went outside for a while each day. My mother preferred the outdoors. She was always planting—flowers, berries, walnut trees. She was a great baker and was especially known for her pies: apple, elderberry, raspberry, lemon chiffon, and coconut cream. She even baked bread weekly for my family well into her nineties.

Two of her favorite recipes follow:

Molasses Crinkles

¾ c. shortening	¼ t. salt
1 c. brown sugar	2 t. soda
1 egg beaten	½ t. cloves
½ c. molasses	1 t. cinnamon
2¼ c. flour	1 t. ginger

Cream shortening and sugar. Beat in egg and molasses. Sift flour with salt, soda, and spices. Add creamed mixture.Chill 1 hour. Shape into balls the size of a walnut. Place on cookie sheet (greased). Brush tops lightly with water and sprinkle with sugar.

Bake at 375°F for 10 min. Makes 36.

Christmas Steamed Pudding

1 egg	2–3 t. sugar
1 c. molasses	1 c. milk
1 c. chopped suet or ½ c. butter	3 c. flour
1 c. raisins	½ t. salt
2 t. soda	½ t. cinnamon, cloves, allspice, nutmeg

Steam in double boiler for 2 ½ hrs.

Pudding Sauce

½ c. sugar	1 t. Flour (cornstarch)
1 t. butter	1 c. boiling water
2 t. vinegar	¼ t. nutmeg

Combine ingredients. Boil until clear.
Double or triple for more sauce.

Even in snowstorms or when it was raining, I would walk down the road to our woods and spend time sitting on a favorite rock, leaning against a tree, looking for changes in the foliage, listening to the birds, picking flowers, or just daydreaming and sorting out everything that was happening. We liked to go outside at night also. Our father, being a hunter, taught us about the sounds of animals and how to track them. We even went coon hunting, squirrel hunting, and bobcat hunting. My sister and I were not as brave as our brother, but we did go outside after dark and listen to the sounds of the woods. My brother grew up to be a big game hunter with trophies from around the world.

For a few years there was a bobcat that stayed around our woods and fields in late summer and early fall. One night we heard its awful screeching about a half-mile behind our house. We knew the path it would take, so my mother, brother, sister and I decided on a plan to get him. He would be crossing the road into our woods in about five minutes. We had a flashlight and a gun and quietly walked in the dark toward our woods. All of a sudden the bobcat let out a screech. He was crossing the road about four hundred feet ahead of us. We turned on the flashlight where we heard the screech. All we saw was a flash of eyes and movement. Within a minute, we heard him screeching way at the back of our woods and then way east, over a mile away. Bobcats are known for their speed in disappearing when being stalked.

This bobcat was the talk of the area and everyone was trying to shoot him. I could shoot a gun, but my brother was an expert marksman. One summer night when we were teens, our parents left us alone. The doors and windows were open and all at once came the familiar scream of the bobcat. My brother and I went onto the front porch and listened carefully to the path the screeching was taking. It seemed to circle around and seemed to be coming straight down the fence line of the pasture across the road from our house. I held a large oversized flashlight as my brother readied his rifle. When the screams were within range, I would turn on the light and Carl would shoot where he saw its eyes shining. Seconds seemed like hours as we waited for the right scream. As planned, I aimed the flashlight where we heard the scream and Carl fired the gun. Then we heard, "moooooo." We both looked at each other and started praying. There hadn't been any cows there this afternoon. Then I shined the light again and we saw several young beef cows stand up in the tall grass and start moving. They had all been lying down. What if we had killed one? How could we ever pay the price of one? We knew they sold for several hundred dollars. What would our parents say? They would never trust us again. We prayed some more. Finally, my brother climbed the fence with the flashlight and looked all around. He checked every cow and could find no injuries. The next day we searched the pasture for a dead one, but none was found. We vowed to each other never to use a gun again when our parents were away. We never told our parents about hearing the bobcat and trying to shoot him. My brother had to give up his dream of being a big game hunter for a few years. The bobcat had outsmarted us again.

Trapping muskrats and mink was another source of extra cash. My brother used to hunt woodchucks in summer and trap muskrats in the winter. I recall rising before 5:00 A.M. one brisk, cold, clear winter morning to go with him to check his two miles of trapping lines along the ditch banks of the Manning Muck. The prey caught was put in a bag, the traps reset, and later the hides were skinned, scraped, and stretched on a board. In late spring, he would sell them—usually to Rush's in Waterport.

I remember being cold all winter long. We lived a mile from the Manning School and in winter it was bitter cold walking home. When a blizzard was blowing we would stop at each house on our route until we were picked up by our parents or we could make it home. The neighbors who saw a lot of the Sherwood children in the winter were: the Mortiers, Bill Copeland, the Mathes, and the Thorpes. They were all kind to us and tried to thaw us out. We would thaw out in one place, get wrapped up with scarves covering our mouths, and trudge on in the storm to the next house. By the time I reached home I felt like I was frozen stiff and lifeless. All I was able to do was to lie next to the pot-bellied stove and fall asleep on the floor.

During World War II we children felt we were part of the war effort. Rural one-room schoolhouses became the collection centers for scrap metal and huge bags of milkweed pods. Supposedly the milkweed fiber was used in parachutes and life jackets. In the fall we roamed the fields filling bags with pods. We were even given time off from school to do this on Friday afternoons.

V-E Day and then V-J Day came in the summer of 1945. It was finally over. The United States and her allies defeated Japan, Italy, and Germany. I recall the bells ringing from every school and church and people lighting bonfires called victory fires. You could hear cannon or firecrackers in the distant towns, as well as their horns, bells, and sirens. We got out of school early. The weeks that followed the liberation of the concentration camps in Europe, my parents were given old copies of *Life* magazine. I remember staring in disbelief at the scenes from the war: scenes of D-Day, June 6, 1944, when the allies stormed the beaches of Normandy, pictures of dead and wounded soldiers, and starving, unclad bodies of gas chamber victims. I had never seen any pictures of war like this before. How could anyone do these things?

With the end of the war the servicemen came home. Some of the neighborhood men worked on road construction. LaVerne Bubb was one of these soldiers. At recess we would wave to him as he worked on 31A in front of the Manning School and he would wave back to us.

Only main roads were paved. In the 1950s our road, Hindsburg, was no longer dirt. I remember sitting on our porch and watching the process of coating the road with tar and stones. A lot of work was needed because America's roads had not been a priority in the war years.

Sometime during the war years, I remember going to the movie theater in Holley to my first movie, *So Dear to My Heart* starring Burl Ives. In school we put pins on a world map for current events. Someone would buy a newspaper and it would be shared with many until it fell apart. We often played war. We prayed for peace in church. We had blackout drills. Kate Smith sang on the radio. "Lili Marlene" became a wartime love song, popular with Americans, British, and Germans.

The Beginning of My Formal Education

Manning School

BECAUSE OF THE HARD WORK AND MANY CHORES AT HOME, school was a very special place for me. Even when school was closed, I played school at home by myself or with my pets. (While growing up we had a dog named Brownie and two Manx cats, Fuzzy and Bobby, given to us by Don Miner. This breed of cat had a short stubby tail.) They didn't mind being my pupils. Manning School or Clarendon #11 was located on Route 31A, one mile from our home. Typical of other rural, one-room schools, it had one large room (approximately twenty by thirty feet) with an attached wood shed. Grades K through six attended, then for seventh grade we were bused to Holley and spent grades seven through twelve at Holley High School. I never saw a library until seventh grade.

Manning School . . . My school . . .
Clarendon #11

We had a set of reference books, an old set of *Encyclopedia Britannica* that no one could understand, a dictionary, and a few historical novels (which the teacher read to us each year). She often borrowed books from area libraries for us to read. While I attended Manning School, there were never more than sixteen pupils at one time in the whole school. Most often the count was ten to fourteen pupils per year. I was the only pupil in my class each year because no one else was my age.

Mrs. Eva Butler was my teacher for those six wonderful years at Manning School. She was a very kind, patient, inspiring woman . . . in my child's eye . . . a saint. There wasn't anything I wouldn't do for her to please her. I liked to stay after school to clean the erasers and wash the blackboards. I liked

The pot bellied stove in the middle of the schoolroom was our friend in winter.

it when she told me I was a good artist and that I would make a good teacher some day. She planted the seed in my mind in those early years that led me to excel artistically and to make education my life's work; first as a teacher, then as a school administrator.

Friday afternoons we had a spelling bee and an art lesson. Sometimes it was a famous artist or the work of one. This art time might often be a combination of several subjects (music, science, poetry, famous people). Sometimes it was illustrating a poem or story we had written. Sometimes it was creating a mural about a historical event. I couldn't wait to be in sixth grade; the only one in my class, I had the whole blackboard to myself. Since we studied medieval days, I fashioned a large castle with towers and a drawbridge as well as knights on horses. It took a long time, but I could work on it when I had all my other work completed. So, on the back of wallpaper taped to the blackboard, I used

The front of the Manning School classroom:
teacher's desk in front, bell rope near door leading to hall.

colored chalk to color my scene. Sometimes, the pupils voted for the best picture to be placed on the bulletin board for a week. I usually had one on display each week. It was about sixth grade when I realized or discovered I could put an image of anything I saw on paper and get a good result or likeness.

Being in sixth grade meant having the whole blackboard in the back of the school as one's pallet. Great, if you were an artist!

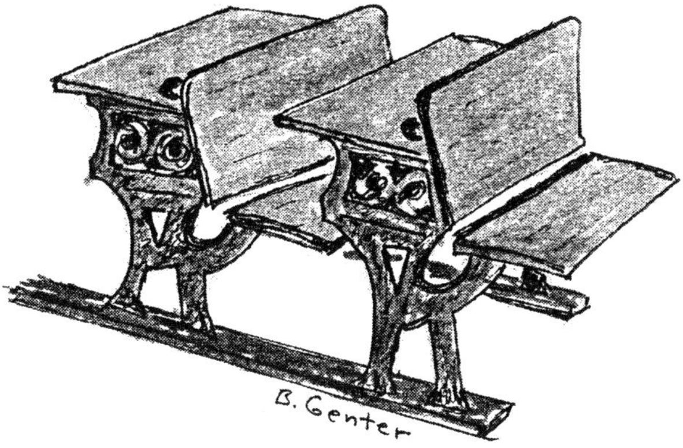

School desks were screwed to skids so a row could be moved all at once.

After high school, I entered Brockport State Teachers College at seventeen, completed their condensed three-year program, and started teaching fifth grade at the Albion Grammar School when I was twenty years old. After seventeen years in the classroom, I became Reading Coordinator, Assistant Superintendent, Principal of Waterport School, Director of Elementary Education and Principal at Albion Middle School. But it all started because of Mrs. Butler's guidance and nudging. As a college student I would stop by and visit her and tell her what I was learning and doing.

I was a determined child. My mother tried to follow doctor's directions by pulling me on a sled and wagon to school and home again, but I would jump off the wagon or sled and run ahead of my brother and sister who were walking. If they could walk, so could I. They were younger than me and I wouldn't let them do anything better than me. This attitude helped me grow up strong and healthy and determined to be an artist and teacher.

We carried our lunches to school in a metal lunch pail. Usually lunch consisted of a peanut butter or fried egg sandwich and an apple. In the winter some of the mothers who lived near the school might make a pot of soup and it would simmer on top of the pot-bellied stove all morning . . . sending delicious aromas into the air. We couldn't wait for lunchtime to come, so we worked harder to pass the morning time away. Sometimes we would take potatoes to school and let them bake on the stovetop. Soup and potatoes were wonderful additions to our lunches on those days.

I have so many special memories of the years spent at Manning School. All summer I longed for school to start. I carefully selected my crayons, pencils, and a Big Chief tablet. In fifth and sixth grade we also needed a spelling and a social studies notebook. Pencil boxes were often made at home. All summer I missed seeing my teacher behind her desk, the smell of chalk, and the interaction with my classmates.

So many memories:

Being very shy, I hardly dared look at all the other children when my parents dropped me off at Manning School on a snowy, late fall day. The little kids sat on the roadside of the schoolroom and the bigger kids in fifth and sixth grades sat to the north. After a few days, I played with everyone and got to know their names. I loved colors and crayons and always colored when my work was finished. I also noticed that Roy Bubb in fifth grade had a beautiful, large selection of colors in his box of crayons; while I had only the standard eight crayons in mine. Mrs. Butler, the teacher, would give us permission to speak in a whisper, to another pupil, while she was hearing a group with its lesson. All we had to do was raise our hand and she would nod her head to give permission.

Manning School Photo—1942

1st Row: Betty Sherwood, Carl Sherwood, Jimmy Gaylord.
2nd Row: Buddy Cook, Richard Bell, Clifford Germeo, Billy Bartlett, Harold Pratt.
3rd Row: Roy Bubb, Clayton Bubb, Ethel Pratt, Joann Kennedy, Mrs. Butler, Lois Bubb.

Halloween Dressup at Manning School—1944

1ST ROW: Joybell Germeo, Jimmy Gaylord, Jimmy's cousin, Dolores Bubb, Billy Bartlett, two unknowns.

2ND ROW: Betty Sherwood (holding her mask), Carl Sherwood (in wig & hat), Howard Bartlett, Harold Pratt, Richard Bell, Clayton Bubb.

3RD ROW: Joann Kennedy, Ethel Pratt.

Manning School—1945

1ST ROW: Dale Cook, Nancy Mortier, Jimmy Gaylord, Joyce Sherwood, Shirley Pratt, Joybell Germeo.

2ND ROW: Carl Sherwood, Clifford Germeo, Mrs. Butler, Lois Bubb, Betty Sherwood, Dolores Bubb.

I couldn't take my eyes off all those bright, wonderful crayons in Roy's possession, so after a few days, I mustered up all the courage I had, and raised my hand. Mrs. Butler nodded her head, "Yes." Leaving my desk and crossing over the front of the room seemed to take forever, but I finally reached Roy's desk. I quietly asked him if I could borrow one of his crayons. He let me. When I finished I took the crayon back and asked to borrow another color. This went on for a day or two. Finally, the teacher talked to me that I should use my own crayons and not bother Roy who had work to do. I made up my mind that some how I would find a box of many colors for next year and have my parents buy them for me.

The only time I ever cheated (tried to cheat) on a test was in fourth grade. As I mentioned before, we could draw when our work was finished. Since I was the only one in my class, I wasn't always checked on . . . I had to work independently most of the time. Our assignments were written on the blackboard. I must have been engrossed in drawing or doing other work because I never saw that the teacher had written that I would have a social studies test the next day. As test time arrived the next morning, the teacher said, "Clear your desk and take out a piece of paper." I panicked as I realized I didn't know about the test and had not studied the material. I looked at the board and sure enough, there was the posted test. As I read through the questions, I panicked more. Then I realized my social studies book was in the front of my desk and all I had to do would be to open it up and look up the answers. I knew where I could find them. Slowly, I eased the book out into my lap and started to turn to the right section. From behind and over my right shoulder came the arm and hand of my teacher and she closed the book. She said, "We don't use the book when taking a test." I was so ashamed; so afraid she would never trust me again. That was probably the only failing mark I got, and I learned that there is a next time. I also learned to check my assignments. I don't remember trying to cheat ever again.

The woodshed became our playground on rainy days. We used our imagination to turn big boxes into a school, an office, a store, or a home. We cut openings for windows and set up furniture. Grocery boxes and empty jars made it a store. We even sold penny candy to the little kids.

On good days at recess and noon, someone would yell, "Let's play ball!" We often made up the rules of the game as we chose sides. The two team leaders used a baseball bat with hand-over-hand to decide which team would go first. Other games we played were: tug of war; kick the can; Annie, Annie, over; hide-and-seek; and prisoner's goal. Sticks were used for bases, and for horses when we played cowboys and indians. Pieces of wood were used

The boys put jump ropes around the girls and rounded them up for Cowboys & Indians. The girls were the cows.

In winter, sleds were brought to school for an hour of play at noon. We tried to extend the time by being far from the school, on South Manning Road, when our time was up.

for guns in cops and robbers and war. The boys put jump ropes around the girls and rounded us up. We were the cows. We didn't mind being chased by the boys this way. I don't remember anyone being roughed up. During the war years no one had extra money for toys. Brooms, sticks, scrap paper and metal, or a piece of rope sparked our imagination and we created our own toys.

In the winter we played fox and geese and brought our sleds to school. We had an extra long playtime because it took so long to dress up in layers of outdoor clothing; and even longer to get out of the wet, snow-covered grab when playtime ended. We thought we were clever at extending the playtime. We would take our sleds way up South Manning Road to slide down the high embankments of snow. The teacher would ring the bell when it was time to come in. We always managed to be the longest possible distance from the school when we knew it was near the end of playtime. By the time we trudged back to the school, helped each other pull off boots and frozen clothes, went to the outhouse, and got a drink of water, we could add on at least fifteen minutes more. I don't think Mrs. Butler ever scolded us for doing this. She probably corrected all her papers while we were gone.

Winter was a time to build great snow forts and tunnels and to have snowball fights or wars. Once my brother was behind the wall of a fort yelling at the other side that they couldn't get him. A snowball from the other side came flying at him—right into his mouth. That shut him up for a few minutes and gave us a laugh.

There was a ditch that ran along the east side of the school along the edge of North Manning Road. In springtime water flowed rapidly, making it ideal for racing boats. We would make boats out of paper, wood, and sticks and sail them by using a long stick to guide them around clumps of soil and debris. It was easy to get wet feet or fall in the water. Those who lived nearby were sent home to change their clothes. The rest of us would have to sit by the stove to dry out.

Every farm and home had a well or two. Water was carried into the houses, barns, and one-room schools for drinking, washing, and cooking. The well pump was a common sight through the 1960s.

Drinking water came from a neighbor's well. The teacher or a large sixth grader would have the job of getting a fresh pail for the day. At first we had only a dipper which everyone used; then we took our own cups to school; and finally, about when I was in fourth grade, people became more health conscious so each school had a water dispenser (a crock with a spigot at the bottom) and we used paper cups to drink from. Someone still had to fill the crock each morning and drain it at night so it wouldn't freeze. It also had to be cleaned.

Jimmy always wanted to ring the morning bell. Finally his chance came. However, the bell had more strength than Jimmy.

The belfry with the school's bell sat on the roof. A thick rope was attached to it and the rope hung through a hole in the ceiling, falling near the door in front of the classroom. It was an honor to be the one to ring the bell each morning. This task usually went to the larger, taller pupils. They took turns. Jimmy Gaylord was a very tiny kindergartner. Every day he would tease the bigger kids to let him ring the bell. Finally, one day we had a substitute teacher. She asked whose turn it was to ring the bell. We all called out, "Jimmy's." With that, Jimmy jumped up, puffed out his chest, reached for the rope, and immediately was swung to the ceiling by the strong pull of the rope. He hung on while crying for help. We were rolling in the aisle with laughter. Finally, the substitute realized she had to act and pulled him down. As he took his seat, we were amazingly quiet, waiting to see if we would be reprimanded. Jimmy waited a few years before he tried to ring the bell again.

The school had a boy's and a girl's outhouse directly behind and attached to the school. A door through the woodshed led to the boy's and a door through the hail led to the girl's. There was a high wooden partition separating the two and they could be entered from the outside as well. Catalogs and magazines were used for toilet paper and wasting time from class. Each summer, a farmer had the job of cleaning them out, sprinkling lime in the holes, and readying them for the next crop of users. In winter we would run to the outhouse without putting on our heavy winter coats, so we didn't stay very long daydreaming.

One day a week a traveling music teacher named Mary Webster would teach us songs as she played the piano. I always looked forward to this. We did plays: Christmas and Patriotic. A sheet was strung across the front of the room on a wire for a stage curtain. You really had to use your imagination in these performances. Our parents would come to watch us sing and dance and

The outhouses were attached to the school by a walkway of cement and a board fence. They were places of intrigue.

say a few lines at an evening performance. We thought we were big time. But it was great fun! It was the only time our parents went to school. I was a shy, quiet child, but I loved playacting.

Girls didn't wear pants or shorts to school. The only time pants were worn was in winter, over or under a dress or skirt, and they were taken off once you got to school. All girls wore brown or black long stockings to keep legs warm in winter. Usually by Easter, all girls were wearing short socks. We hated the long stockings because they would twist around your legs and they were always baggy at the knees. At the first hint of warm weather, the older girls would come to school, go to the outhouse, unhook their stockings from their garter belts, and roll their stockings down to their ankles. Before they went home they would fasten them back up to the garter belt so their mothers' wouldn't know. Our mothers were afraid we would be cold and get sick if we gave up the heavy stockings before the weather was really mild and warm. I loved colors, especially bright-colored boys' socks. I could not understand why boys' socks were so pretty and girls' socks came only in plain colors. So for a few years, between ten and thirteen, I insisted on wearing striped socks, even on Easter Sunday.

Each spring and fall, on a nice warm, sunny day, we would head for the woods, one half-mile north of the school, on North Manning Road. The teacher would go with the younger children while the bigger ones ran ahead. We took our lunches and found a sunny spot to eat, in or near the woods. After lunch we went off in groups to collect flowers, leaves, and anything else we wanted. On the west edge of the woods was a broken-down, abandoned house. The older kids told the younger kids the house was haunted. As an older kid, with three friends, I decided to check it out. We crept onto the fallen-in porch, pulled open the creaky door, adjusted our eyes to the darkness, and looked around. We saw the door to the basement and wondered what was down there. The boys dared us to go down the steps to see. As I started down the first step, I could make out a pile of bones and skulls on the floor below. I turned and ran up the steps and outside as fast as I could. On the way back to school and for many recesses after, we four would huddle together and talk in whispers about what we had seen and tried to figure out if the house was really haunted or not. It was a real scary topic for at least a year. I had dreams about the place. About a year later, a friend of my father's was at our house talking hunting. I happened to hear their conversation about a former dog catcher who would roundup stray dogs and take them to this "haunted house," shoot them, and collect a bounty for his deed. Now the mystery was solved. The bones and skulls were from poor lost dogs that no one wanted.

More Diversions From Work

Barns were fascinating places to play. The barns around and on the muckland were more like sheds where bushel baskets, crates, and machinery were kept. But we played in them anyway. When we rented Ed Murphy's muck, which was to the south, across a ditch from our piece of land, there was a very small house (maybe twenty by twenty feet), near the road on the Murphy property. Its windows had been broken out and there were no doors. While it was in this state we played in it every chance we got. There were two tiny rooms downstairs, a narrow staircase to the low-ceilinged hip roof upstairs, with two tiny spaces for bedrooms. In the larger space upstairs, was an old, broken-down bed, an old mattress, and a dirty old blanket. We would imagine that we lived in the house and told how nice it would be, fixed up, and where our pieces of furniture would go. Sometimes, we would play cards on the floor. One evening, we rode our bikes there and went upstairs. An old window frame was in the way on the floor, so we threw it onto the bed and continued our play. The next day we went there to play again and had a surprise. The window frame was on the floor again. Again, we threw it onto the bed. The next day, and for several days after, the frame would be on the floor. We had purposely put it on the bed each night. This remained a mystery until one day we saw a strange man, a "bum," come out of the house and walk down the road. Apparently he was working for an area farmer and was "homeless" so he used our little playhouse as a motel each night.

After we told our parents about the bum living in the house, my father put glass in the windows, replaced the doors, and put a lock on it to secure it. He stored fertilizer and seeds inside for several years. We couldn't play in it any more. Time went by. I went to college; other people worked the muck and my father passed away. Someone bought the little house and moved it on sledges up the Mansfield Road and around the corner toward Shepherd's Sawmill, run by Graydon Stymus. They placed it on the west side of Transit Road and built on to it so a family could live in it.

I liked to be at my grandmother's farm on Hulberton Road in Clarendon when my cousins were there. The barns were huge and in many different shapes. Haying season was the best. I remember the giant team of horses that was hitched to a tow-rope that extended from the barn. Slings were under and around the wagonload of hay in the barn. When the horses were given the signal, they walked out away from the barn, pulling the rope that lifted the load of hay to the mow above. Someone pulled another rope from inside the barn to swing the mass of hay to one side of the mow and then tripped the forks holding it so that the hay fell where it was supposed to. Even when I was very young, my uncle would lift me onto the back of one of the horses and let me sit on the horse as he worked. When I was a little bigger, I got to lead (walk) the horses to the end of the rope.

My older boy cousins tried to use the sling mechanism for play; lifting each other up, swinging onto the piles of hay in the loft. They were lucky not to have been hurt. If the rope had been tripped in mid-air, the one holding on would have crashed many feet to the cement floor below. We had all been warned not to play with the slings and what could happen, but it had to be tested by the boys. It was great fun to slide down the hay chutes to the cow mangers below, to milk a cow, to climb to the top of the silo. We always played hide and seek all over the barns.

Another wonderful set of barns to play in was the four barns on the Bubb farm. You could hide forever and no one would find you. I was very good at playing hide and seek and never being caught. You see I was very skinny and learned that if I could get my head through an opening, then I could hunch in my shoulders and slide right through. The best place to use this technique was behind our house. I would run through the grass, slide through a section of pasture fence and crawl a long way in the grass. I did have nightmares about lions creeping up on me in the grass.

Across from Manning School was Jim Gaylord's Gas Station; a very tiny building with a canopy over the two gas pumps outside. It was a big treat to go inside to spend a penny or two on gum or candy. Once in a while my mother would run out of bread at home and would give one of us (usually me) a dime to buy a loaf of Wonder Bread. If you were lucky enough to have a nickel you could buy a Clark, Snickers, or Hershey Bar. Also inside were oil for cars and tobacco and cigarettes. There was only room for four or five adults to stand around the stove. In the winter it was crowded as men came in to warm up. In the 1950s a soda pop cooler was added and gave us one more reason to want to go there in warm weather. We felt grown-up when we were allowed to purchase something from Jim's Gas Station.

TOP: Jim Gaylord's gas station, located across from the Manning School, was a fascinating place for a child.
BOTTOM: Jim Gaylord's gas station on Rt. 31A, as it appeared in 2002 as a residence.

From the age of ten on, my brother, sister, and I had our own individual garden spot north of our house. I was in an individual 4-H Club from then until I was fifteen. My garden was my project as well as rabbits one year. I took good care of my garden so I would have a lot of vegetables to display at the

Orleans County Fair in August. I still have a scrapbook full of the ribbons I won. All summer we looked forward to going to the Fair. When we were little we had to stay with our mother, but by twelve years old we were allowed to go off by ourselves for the day's events. The fair grounds then were at the end of West State Street in Albion where the Fireman's Recreational Hall now stands. Years ago I remember the racetrack and the races we watched from the grandstand. We could pet the horses when they weren't racing. There were barns full of chickens, rabbits, cows, sheep, and pigs. There was a two-story building where clothing, baked goods, and vegetables were displayed. The rides were in a separate section. It was at the age of twelve, I worked up enough courage to ride the Ferris wheel for the first time, with a boy. Sometimes there were parades around the racetrack, with decorated pony carts, clowns, old trucks and cars, acrobats doing stunts, and jugglers. There was always something going on. And, of course, lots of food to sample. We didn't have much money, but we had saved all summer for the Fair. If we were lucky, our parents would take us for two days. There were also sideshows and the crazy glass house. At twelve years old you just knew you were growing up when you got lost in the crowd at the Fair, met up with other boys and girls and took in the events. Several times we sat on the grass next to our car, ate our lunch, and discussed life's mysteries.

When I had finished high school and gone off to college, Lee Bowen helped my father with harvesting, cutting brush along the road, plumbing jobs, and went hunting with him. He remembers starting the fire in the storage to keep the produce from freezing when the temperature dropped to thirty-two degrees or lower. It was his job to watch the temperature and go out to the storage and keep fuel on the fire. Dad would come there later in the day and they would sit around the stove, talking hunting and life.

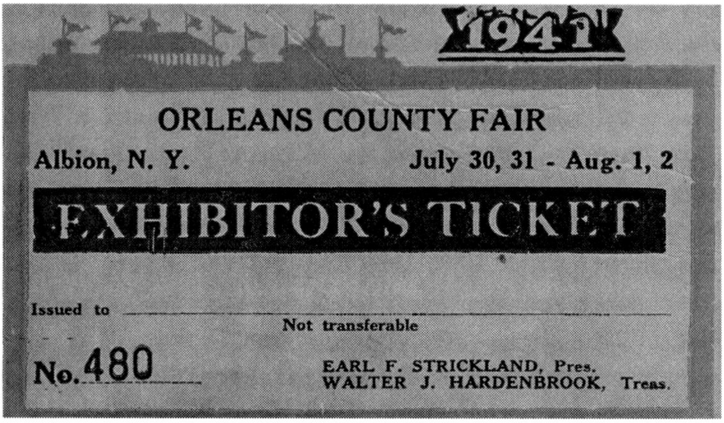

The Orleans County Fair was a summer event looked forward to by all people . . . young and old.

When doing a plumbing job, they would go to Holley to get the supplies and always go to Wolcott's Dairy to get a milkshake.

Yes, growing up on a muckland farm in the 1940s and the 1950s was a learning experience few children could comprehend today. Money was scarce, everyone worked, shared, cooperated. No one had to tell or show us how to get along with other children. I do not remember many arguments leading to fights.

You needed friends. There weren't that many others your age around, so you found a way to get along and accepted each one's differences. Even though I was shy and self-conscious about the way I walked with a limp, I don't recall others taunting or teasing me about it. If we were playing cowboys, I might be called, "Hop-a-long," but it was in good spirit with the game. Besides, Hopalong Cassidy was a great cowboy hero in the movies.

Adults shared their food, time, skills, and machinery with each other. Children were always with their parents and learned early in life the same survival skills their parents had learned from their parents. After World War II ended, America began to rebuild and everyone started to have more material things, more money to spend, and even started looking at the world as a much bigger space than the close-knit community everyone knew and was used to during the war years.

By the end of the 1950s, some of the muckland was being deserted and left to grow back into wilderness. Small farmers sold out to larger operators. It became difficult to hire help. No one wanted to do that kind of work any more. This included me. Off to college I went, full of faith and optimism, to finish growing up. However, I shall never forget how I got there . . . with the sacrifices made by my parents and a strong will which I inherited from them.

Betty Sherwood Genter

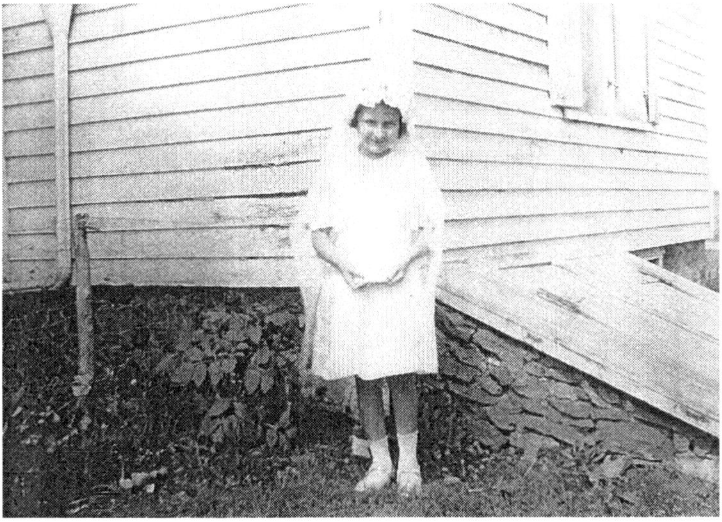

OPPOSITE TOP: The family homestead at 4578 Hindsburg Road, as it appeared in 2002. OPPOSITE MIDDLE: The dormered, right side of this home was our little 20' by 20' play house. It was moved on skids from the Murphy Muck to the west side of Transit Rd. and added onto. As seen in 2002. OPPOSITE BOTTOM: Dad's 1937 Chevy truck, sitting in a field, abandoned, in 1998. TOP: Uncle Ray Bowen with team of horses Betty sat on and later led on a rope during haying season on grandparents' farm. BOTTOM: First Communion for Betty Sherwood, age 6, June 1942.

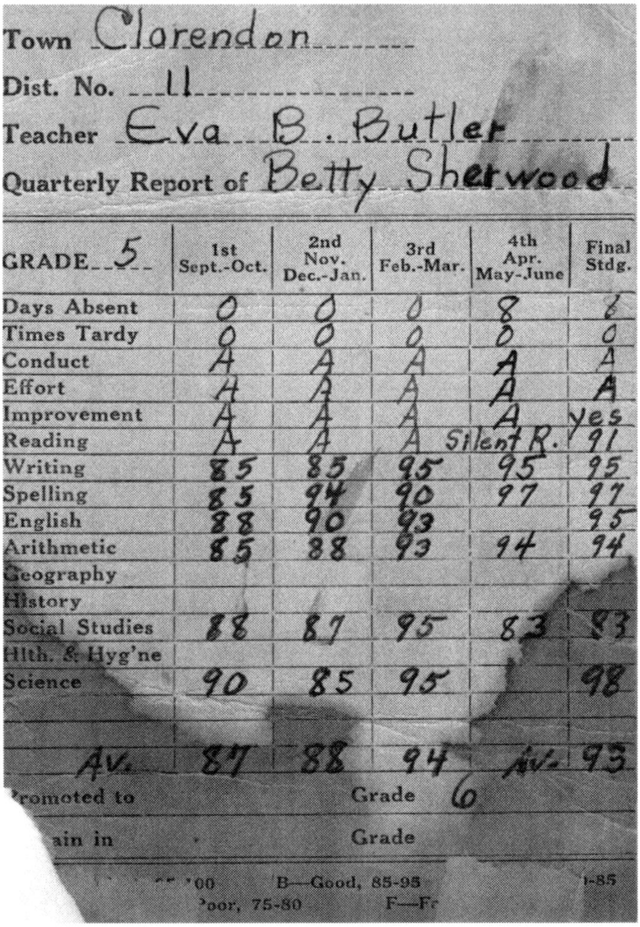

Town Clarendon

Dist. No. 11

Teacher Eva B. Butler

Quarterly Report of Betty Sherwood

GRADE 5	1st Sept.-Oct.	2nd Nov. Dec.-Jan.	3rd Feb.-Mar.	4th Apr. May-June	Final Stdg.
Days Absent	0	0	0	8	8
Times Tardy	0	0	0	0	0
Conduct	A	A	A	A	A
Effort	A	A	A	A	A
Improvement	A	A	A	A	yes
Reading	A	A	A	Silent R.	91
Writing	85	85	95	95	95
Spelling	85	94	90	97	97
English	88	90	93		95
Arithmetic	85	88	93	94	94
Geography					
History					
Social Studies	88	87	95	83	83
Hlth. & Hyg'ne					
Science	90	85	95		98
Av.	87	88	94	Av.	93

romoted to Grade 6

ain in Grade

00 B—Good, 85-95 -85

oor, 75-80 F—F

Betty Sherwood Genter's 5th grade report card from Manning School. Betty became a 5th grade teacher.

Breinigsville, PA USA
17 March 2011
257863BV00001B/2/P

9 780533 163892